EXPLORE THE U.S.A.

TEXAS

Laura Pratt

LET'S READ
AV2 BY WEIGL™
ADDED VALUE • AUDIO VISUAL

AV² provides enriched content that supplements and complements this book. Weigl's AV² boo strive to create inspired learning and engage young minds in a total learning experience.

Your AV² Media Enhanced books come alive with...

Audio
Listen to sections of
the book read aloud.

Key Words
Study vocabulary, and
complete a matching
word activity.

Video
Watch informative
video clips.

Quizzes
Test your knowledge.

Embedded Weblinks
Gain additional information
for research.

Slide Show
View images and
captions, and prepare
a presentation.

Try This!
Complete activities and
hands-on experiments.

... and much, much more

Go to **www.av2books.com**,
and enter this book's
unique code.

BOOK CODE

N 3 2 9 0 7 9

AV² **by Weigl** brings you media
enhanced books that support
active learning.

Published by AV² by Weigl
350 5th Avenue, 59th Floor
New York, NY 10118
Website: www.av2books.com   www.weigl.com

Library of Congress Cataloging-in-Publication Data

Pratt, Laura.
 Texas / Laura Pratt
   p. cm. -- (Explore the U.S.A.)
 Includes bibliographical references and index.
 ISBN 978-1-61913-407-2 (hard cover : alk. paper)
 1. Texas--Juvenile literature. I. Title.
 F386.3.P72 2013
 976.4--dc23
                              2012016271

Printed in the United States of America in North Mankato, Minnesota
1 2 3 4 5 6 7 8 9 16 15 14 13 12

052012
WEP040512

Project Coordinator: Karen Durrie
Art Director: Terry Paulhus

Weigl acknowledges Getty Images as the primary
image supplier for this title.

Pages 12–13

The current Lone Star flag was adopted as the official flag of Texas in 1839. The star is a tribute to the state's independence from Mexico. The colors of the Texas flag are the same as the colors of the American flag. The blue stands for loyalty, the white represents purity, and the red symbolizes bravery.

Pages 14–15

The longhorn is a type of cattle known for producing lean beef. The longhorn is the official animal of the University of Texas at Austin. All of its sports teams share the name. The nine-banded armadillo is the only species of armadillo in the United States. It is a nocturnal mammal that uses its long nose to find ants and termites to eat.

Pages 16–17

Austin is the capital city of Texas. Austin is the fourth-largest city in Texas. It sits on the bank of the Colorado River. A city law states that buildings in Austin cannot be taller than the capitol building. The city hosts a large music festival every year called South by Southwest. Austin is called the live music capital of the world.

Pages 18–19

The King Ranch covers an area of 825,000 acres (333,866 hectares). Texas is sometimes called "cotton country" because of the amount of cotton that is grown there. Texas produces more cotton than any other state.

Pages 20–21

Many rodeos are held across Texas every year. One of the biggest rodeos is the Houston Livestock Show and Rodeo. This three-week-long rodeo attracts more than two million people each year. One of the best-known tourist destinations in Texas is the Alamo, the ruins of a famous 1836 battle.

KEY WORDS

Research has shown that as much as 65 percent of all written material published in English is made up of 300 words. These 300 words cannot be taught using pictures or learned by sounding them out. They must be recognized by sight. This book contains 66 common sight words to help young readers improve their reading fluency and comprehension. This book also teaches young readers several important content words, such as proper nouns. These words are paired with pictures to aid in learning and improve understanding.

Page	Sight Words First Appearance
4	for, is, it, its, named, on, state, the, this
7	and, four, in, of, part, where
8	a, after, at, be, country, later, once, one, own, to, took, place, was
11	all, along, an, around, grows, has, over, points, with
12	left, three, white
15	animals, feet, hard, have, long, may, other, small, two
16	also, city, live, many
19	any, are, farms, larger, more, than, there
20	about, come, from, learn, people, see

Page	Content Words First Appearance
4	flag, lone star, Texas
7	Gulf of Mexico, Mexico, shape, United States
11	battle, bluebonnet, fields, flower, oak branch, olive branch, roads, seal
12	color, stripes
15	armadillo, horns, longhorn, shell
16	Austin, lakes, music
19	cattle ranches, Rhode Island
20	cowboys, culture, history, Houston Aquarium, rodeos

24

TEXAS

Contents

2   AV² Book Code
4   Nickname
6   Location
8   History
10 Flower and Seal
12 Flag
14 Animals
16 Capital
18 Goods
20 Fun Things to Do
22 Facts
24 Key Words

This is Texas.
It is called the Lone Star State.
Texas is named for the single star
on its flag.

This is the shape of Texas. It is in the south part of the United States.

Where is Texas?

Canada

United States

Pacific Ocean

Atlantic Ocean

Mexico   Gulf of Mexico

N
W   E
S

Texas borders Mexico, the Gulf of Mexico, and four states.

Texas was once a part of Mexico. Texas later became its own country.

Texas fought to be its own country. One battle took place at the Alamo.

The bluebonnet is the state flower of Texas. This flower grows in fields and along roads all over the state.

The Texas state seal has a star with five points.

Around the star is an oak branch and an olive branch.

This is the state flag of Texas. It has a single star on the left and three stripes of color.

The Texas state flag is red, white, and blue.

Texas has two state animals. One state animal is the armadillo. This is a small animal with a hard shell. The other state animal is the Texas longhorn.

A longhorn may have horns 8 feet long.

The capital city of Texas is Austin. It is in the south part of Texas. Austin is known for its many lakes.

Austin is also known for its live music.

Texas has more farms than any other state. There are also many cattle ranches in Texas.

One ranch in Texas is larger than the state of Rhode Island.

Texas is known for its cowboys, ranches, and rodeos. People come from all over the country to learn about the state's history and culture.

People also come to see the Houston Aquarium.

TEXAS FACTS

These pages provide detailed information that expands on the interesting facts found in the book. These pages are intended to be used by adults as a learning support to help young readers round out their knowledge of each state in the *Explore the U.S.A.* series.

Pages 4–5

In 1836, a flag with a single star in the center became the official flag of the Republic of Texas. The flag's design was changed in 1839, but it still featured a single star. Texas has been represented by the Lone Star flag ever since. Texas is named for the Caddo American Indian word *thecas*, which means "friends."

Pages 6–7

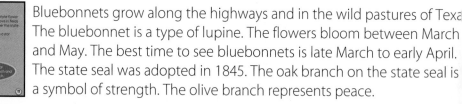

On December 29, 1845, Texas joined the United States as the 28th state. is in the southeastern United States. It borders Mexico to the south and Gulf of Mexico to the southeast. In the north, Texas is bordered by Oklah and Arkansas. To the east, it is bordered by Louisiana. New Mexico share Texas's west border. Texas also has three large islands in the Gulf of Mex

Pages 8–9

American Indians were the first people to live in Texas. Spain was the first country to claim ownership of the land. Before Texas was an American state, it was a Mexican state. After winning its independence from Mexico, Texas was its own country for 10 years.

Pages 10–11

Bluebonnets grow along the highways and in the wild pastures of Texa The bluebonnet is a type of lupine. The flowers bloom between March and May. The best time to see bluebonnets is late March to early April. The state seal was adopted in 1845. The oak branch on the state seal is a symbol of strength. The olive branch represents peace.